Immigration

Debra J. Housel, M.S.Ed.

Publishing Credits

Historical Consultant
Shannon C. McCutchen

Editors
Wendy Conklin, M.A.
Torrey Maloof

Editorial Director
Emily R. Smith, M.A.Ed.

Editor-in-Chief
Sharon Coan, M.S.Ed.

Creative Director
Lee Aucoin

Illustration Manager
Timothy J. Bradley

Publisher
Rachelle Cracchiolo, M.S.Ed.

Teacher Created Materials
5301 Oceanus Drive
Huntington Beach, CA 92649-1030
http://www.tcmpub.com
ISBN 978-0-7439-0662-3

Made in Malaysia
Thumbprints.22065

Table of Contents

Migrating to America

Imagine living in an overcrowded country. There are few jobs and many people are poor and without hope. Some are even **harassed** (huh-RASD) because of their beliefs. Hunger and desperation are everywhere. Wars abound. This was the case during the late nineteenth and early twentieth centuries. So, millions of people **migrated** to the United States. They came from around the world. At no other time in history have so many people flocked to one nation.

America was seen as the land of opportunity. Europe was overcrowded. The people in Europe heard there were jobs and lots of land for farms across the ocean. People left behind everything to come to the United States. Often they sold all they owned to buy tickets. This made their choice **irrevocable** (ir-REH-vuh-kuh-buhl).

Huge crowds of people entered the United States daily. They hoped to get jobs and own homes. They wanted to worship in their own ways and live happy lives. Many had their hopes fulfilled. Others were not so lucky.

Immigrants arriving in the United States wait in line at Ellis Island.

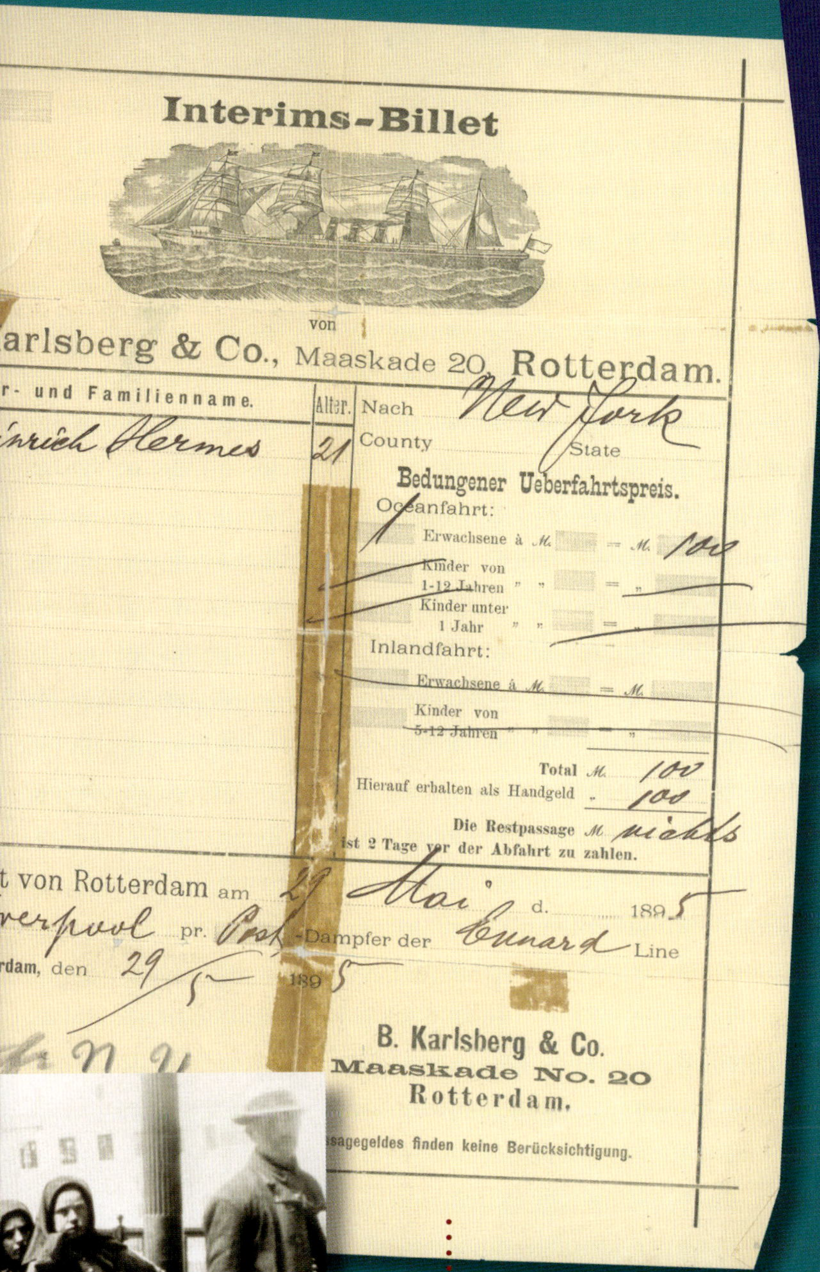

Interims-Billet

von

...arlsberg & Co., Maaskade 20, Rotterdam.

...r- und Familienname. | Alter. | Nach New York | County | State

Bedungener Ueberfahrtspreis.

Oceanfahrt:

Erwachsene à M. = M. 100

Kinder von 1-12 Jahren " " = "

Kinder unter 1 Jahr " " = "

Inlandfahrt:

Erwachsene à M. = M.

Kinder von 5-12 Jahren " " = "

Total M. 100

Hierauf erhalten als Handgeld " 100

Die Restpassage M. nichts

ist 2 Tage vor der Abfahrt zu zahlen.

...t von Rotterdam am 29 Mai d. 1895

...verpool pr. Post-Dampfer der Cunard Line

...rdam, den 29/5 1895

B. Karlsberg & Co.

Maaskade No. 20

Rotterdam.

...sagegeldes finden keine Berücksichtigung.

This is a ship ticket that was used to bring someone to the United States.

The Invitation

In 1883, Emma Lazarus wrote a poem that is now displayed on the Statue of Liberty's base. It reflects what was happening at that time:

"Give me your tired, your poor, your huddled masses **yearning** to breathe free, the wretched **refuse** (REF-yoos) of your teeming shore. Send these, the homeless, **tempest-tost** to me; I lift my lamp beside the golden door!"

Population Explosion

Prior to 1820, no one kept immigration records. In the 1840s about 100,000 people came to the United States each year. By 1854, that figure had quadrupled. By 1860, four million **immigrants** had already entered the nation. And this was before the Great Migration years of 1900–1930.

Before Ellis Island

The Ellis Island station opened in 1892. Prior to that, eight million immigrants came through Castle Island, a huge round stone fort off New York City's shore.

That's a Lot of People!

More than 27 million immigrants entered the United States between 1870 and 1916. The peak year was 1907 when 1.2 million people **immigrated** to the country. Today, one out of every three U.S. citizens has an **ancestor** who came through Ellis Island.

Doctors inspect female immigrants at Ellis Island.

HOLLAND-AMERICA LINE.
Inspection Card
(Third Class Passengers)
Port of departure ROTTERDAM
Date of departure: 26 SEP 1923
Name of Ship RYNDAM
Name of Passenger Barbara Vitkiene
Last residence Lithuania
EASTERN EUROPE
Inspected and passed at Rotterdam
UNITED STATES PUBLIC HEALTH SERVICE
Seal or Stamp of Consular or Medical Officer.
Passed at quarantine, port of , U. S. (Date).
Passed by immigration Bureau, port of (Date).
Berth No. 5 6
To be punched by ship's surgeon at daily inspection

Immigrant inspection card given out at Ellis Island

Entering Ellis Island

Millions of immigrants came to the Ellis Island station. It is near the Statue of Liberty in New York Harbor. At Ellis Island, people had to pass medical and oral tests. Inspectors rejected those who were ill, insane, or had spent time in jail.

People were asked to give their names. Some people had no last names. They gave their first names and what they did for a living. That's how people got the last names of Baker, Cook, and Gardener. Others said what they had been called in their small towns. "Vilhelm John's son" was recorded as "William Johnson." Others changed their own last names. They wanted to hide their **ethnicities** (eth-NIS-uh-teez). They feared the same bad treatment that had driven them from their homes. Many people's names were changed forever.

Most people spent about four hours in the station. Doctors checked them for health problems. The doctors made a chalk mark on a person's shoulder if illness was suspected. The marked people were then looked at more closely.

Immigrant identification card for a man from Peru.

Excluded...The Dreaded Word

The immigrants had to answer questions. This was hard because there were not always **interpreters** (in-TUHR-pruh-tuhrz). And, few immigrants spoke English. This made communication difficult. Some inspectors demanded to see some money. The inspectors wanted to make sure they were not letting beggars into their country.

Each immigrant had to prove that he or she could work. But they could not say they already had a job. Anyone who said that was sent home. The government did not want employers to bring in foreign labor. That would take away jobs from U.S. citizens.

Once the tests were done, about two percent of the people were **excluded**. This meant that they could not enter the nation. They had to get on a ship and go back to their home countries. If a child was excluded, at least one parent had to leave, too. In this way, some families were split up. They never saw each other again.

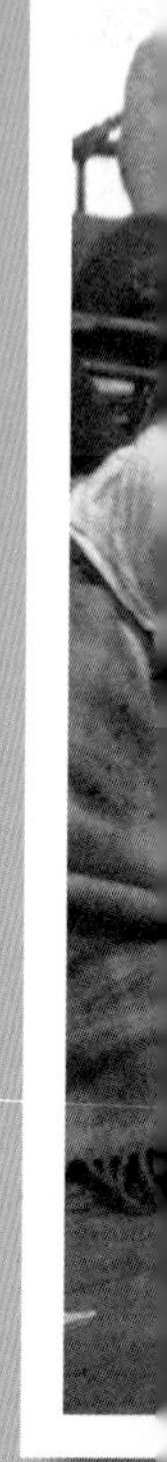

A group of immigrant women and children arrive in the United States.

Detained!

Some people were **detained** at Ellis Island. They were put in detention rooms. These rooms were overcrowded. Sometimes 2,500 people were stuffed into a space meant to hold no more than 1,500.

Meet Me

Single women and children had special rules. They could not leave the island until a male relative claimed them or they got a telegram stating men would meet them at their final destinations.

Immigrants answering questions at Ellis Island

An Italian mother and her three children arrive at Ellis Island.

Africans were taken from their homes by force and sold as slaves in the Americas.

Unwilling Immigrants

Most Africans did not choose to **emigrate**. Millions were kidnapped and taken overseas. Then they were sold into slavery.

Coffin Ships

Conditions were terrible on some ships coming to America. The worst were the Irish "coffin ships." Many people were ill or starving when they boarded. They were told to bring their own food, but they had none to bring! About 16 percent of the passengers died during these horrible voyages.

These Irish peasants have very little food to eat.

Desperate to Live a Better Life

The Irish suffered a **famine** (FAM-uhn) from 1845–1850. Most of the people were already poor. Their main food source was potatoes. When the crops failed, one-fourth of the whole nation starved. Even those with food had problems. Heartless landlords raised the rent on farmers' properties. The farmers could not afford to stay. In addition, most Irish were Roman Catholic. They had to give 10 percent of their **meager** (MEE-gur) income to the church. It was hard to survive.

The Chinese had a rigid class system. Most people were poor. Many of them were starving, too. There were just too many people. But the ruler would not let men leave the country. Chinese men had to sneak aboard ships. If they were caught, they faced death. The Chinese were lured by the gold rush in California in 1849. More men left China when word came that laborers were needed for the railroads and the mines.

This chart shows the number of immigrants living in the United States in 1920. Each man on the chart represents a different country.

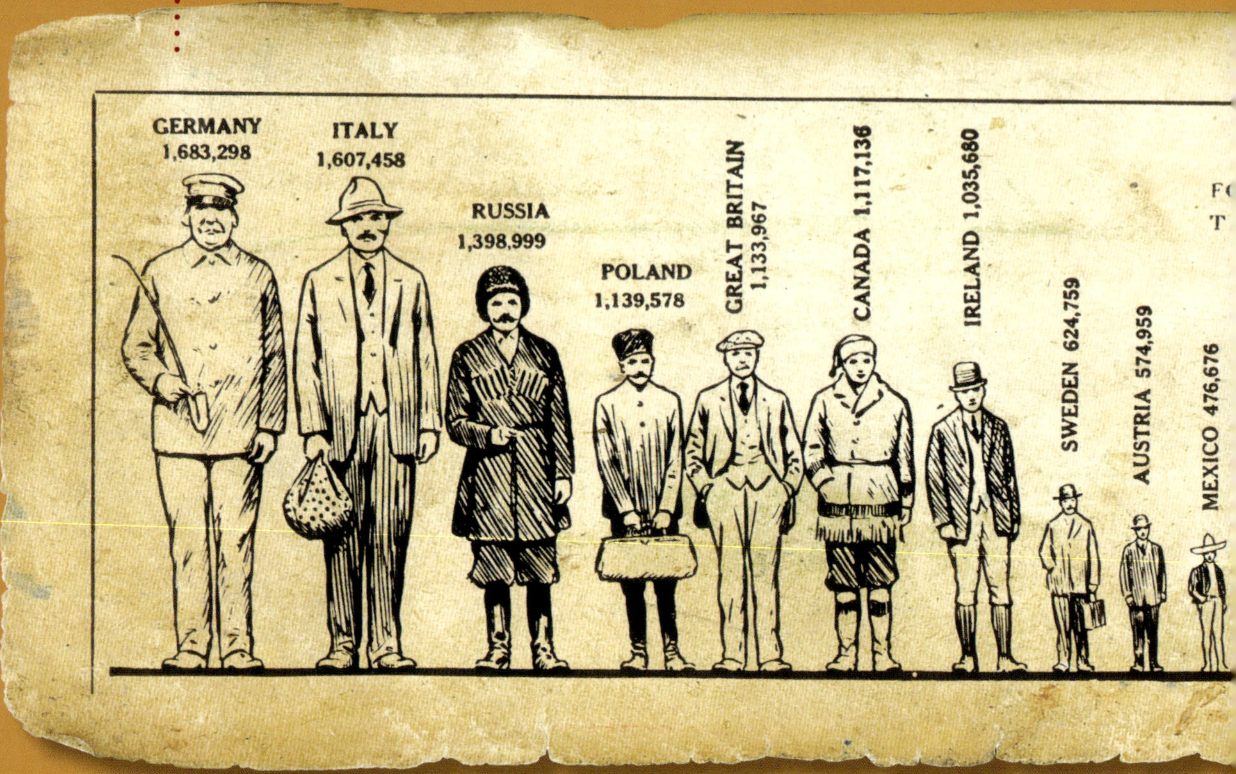

Wars and Free Land

The Crimean (kri-MEE-uhn) War happened in the 1850s. It involved Great Britain, France, Russia, Turkey, and the Ukraine. People fled these war-torn areas.

Other wars caused immigrants to come to the United States, too. During the Mexican Revolution (1910–1920), about 700,000 Mexicans moved across the border. And in Europe, World War I (1914–1918) left many people with nothing. They hoped to start new lives in the United States.

The Homestead Act of 1862 drew people from Germany and Scandinavia. In those nations, land was scarce and owned only by the rich. Free land was as thrilling to them as winning the lottery is to people today.

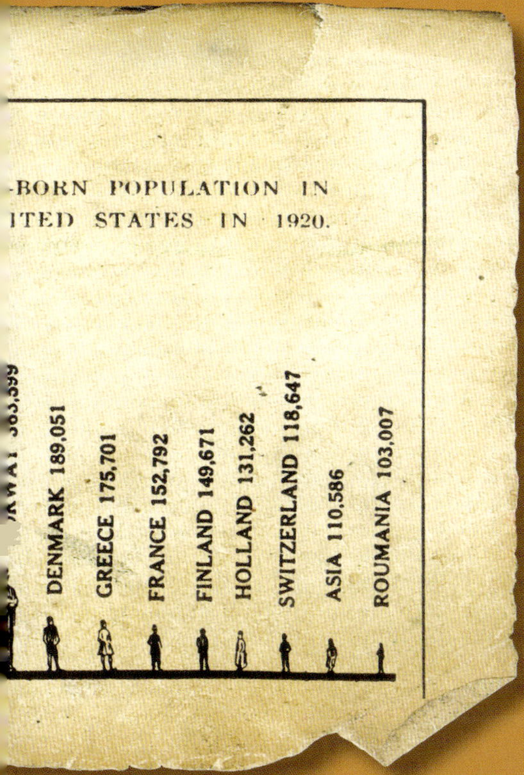

This Mexican immigrant is arriving in the United States.

Lots of Immigrants

Germany sent the most immigrants. The second largest group came from Italy. Italy had too many people, and there were not enough jobs.

Homestead Act

The United States government wanted to encourage people to move west. For a small filing fee, 160 acres (65 hectacres) was given to anyone willing to farm the land. After farming the land for five years, the person owned it. This free land helped Americans and immigrants move west and build their own homes.

The Jewish people in Russia and eastern Europe had nothing to lose. Between 1881 and 1906, **pogroms** (POH-gruhms), or massacres, were backed by brutal leaders. Jewish people were killed by the thousands. They could not have government jobs, own land, or travel. Jewish people were even made to live in certain villages. Without warning, soldiers swept into those towns. They burned homes and beat people. These people wanted safety in a new land.

Tenement life was difficult.

Millions of Men

The majority of immigrants in the late 1800s were men aged 24 to 45. Some men planned to stay just long enough to earn money to improve their lives. Others planned to have their families join them in the United States.

Immigrant Laborers

Many immigrants were miners who worked with coal, copper, and zinc from the earth. Some worked in marble and granite quarries. A quarry is a hole dug into the earth. Others labored as lumberjacks or in steel mills. By 1910, more than half of all of America's industrial workers were immigrants.

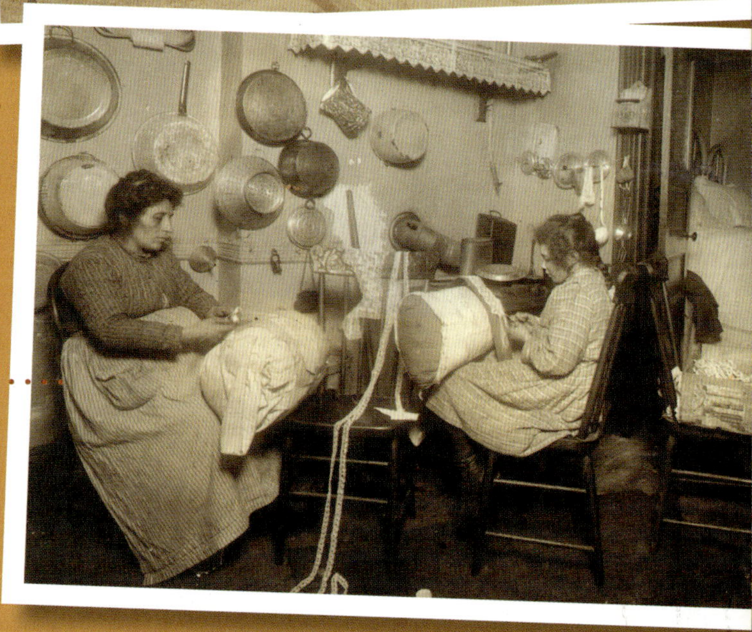

A mother and daughter work in the kitchen of their tenement apartment.

It's So Hard Starting Over

Starting a new life in America was hard. The immigrants faced big problems. At the entry stations, some **crooked** (KROOK-uhd) officials demanded bribes. To get the immigrants to pay, they threatened to exclude family members. On the streets, **swindlers** (SWIND-luhrz) exchanged immigrants' foreign currency for far less than it was worth in U.S. dollars. The immigrants did not know any better. They had to change their money in order to buy things.

Most immigrants lived in **tenements** (TEN-uh-muhnts). Greedy landlords owned these run-down buildings. As many as 32 families were crammed into buildings that lacked air and sunlight. About 4,000 immigrants lived on each city block.

Finding work was easy. But the pay was poor and the conditions were horrible. Business owners did not care if their workers had dirty and hazardous conditions. Industries **exploited** (eks-PLOIT-uhd) immigrant labor. They paid male immigrants less than other workers. Female immigrants earned even less than the male immigrants.

This tenement home shows how poor some immigrants were at this time.

Trying to Fit In

Sometimes whole families worked in their one-room apartments. Instead of going to school, children worked, too. Families did **piecework** for pennies. Piecework included sewing seams or stitching small items together. The immigrants were paid for every piece they completed.

Most immigrants would work in any conditions for long hours and low pay. This made other workers dislike them. American workers felt that they could never improve conditions and wages. Why? There was always a flow of new people willing to put up with anything just to have a job.

There were also language and cultural barriers. Immigrants had to adjust fast. They had to learn English without training. Most children learned the new language faster than the adults did. As they acquired English skills, many children took on decision-making roles in their families.

Some immigrants clung to their own traditions and clothing. At times, they were attacked due to the way they spoke, looked, or dressed. So for comfort, immigrants from each nation clustered in neighborhoods. That's how places like Little Italy and Chinatown formed in big cities.

Clusters of Immigrants

In 1900, the majority of immigrants lived in one of these cities: New York City, Boston, Philadelphia, Detroit, Cleveland, Baltimore, or Chicago.

Catholic Schools

Most of the people who had settled the first colonies were Protestants. Many Catholics feared sending their children to public school because they would be teased or hurt. So they pooled their money and built their own schools.

Mullberry Street was a busy street in an Italian immigrant neighborhood in New York City.

Fear of Immigrants

A lot of U.S. citizens feared that Europe would send its most undesirable people to America. They pictured nations emptying their jails and **insane asylums** (uh-SY-luhmz) onto ships headed for the United States.

Japanese Immigration

Many Japanese people came to Hawaii to work on sugar plantations. Unlike the Chinese government, Japan's leaders encouraged them to go. Between 1886 and 1911, more than 400,000 Japanese men arrived in Hawaii or on the West Coast.

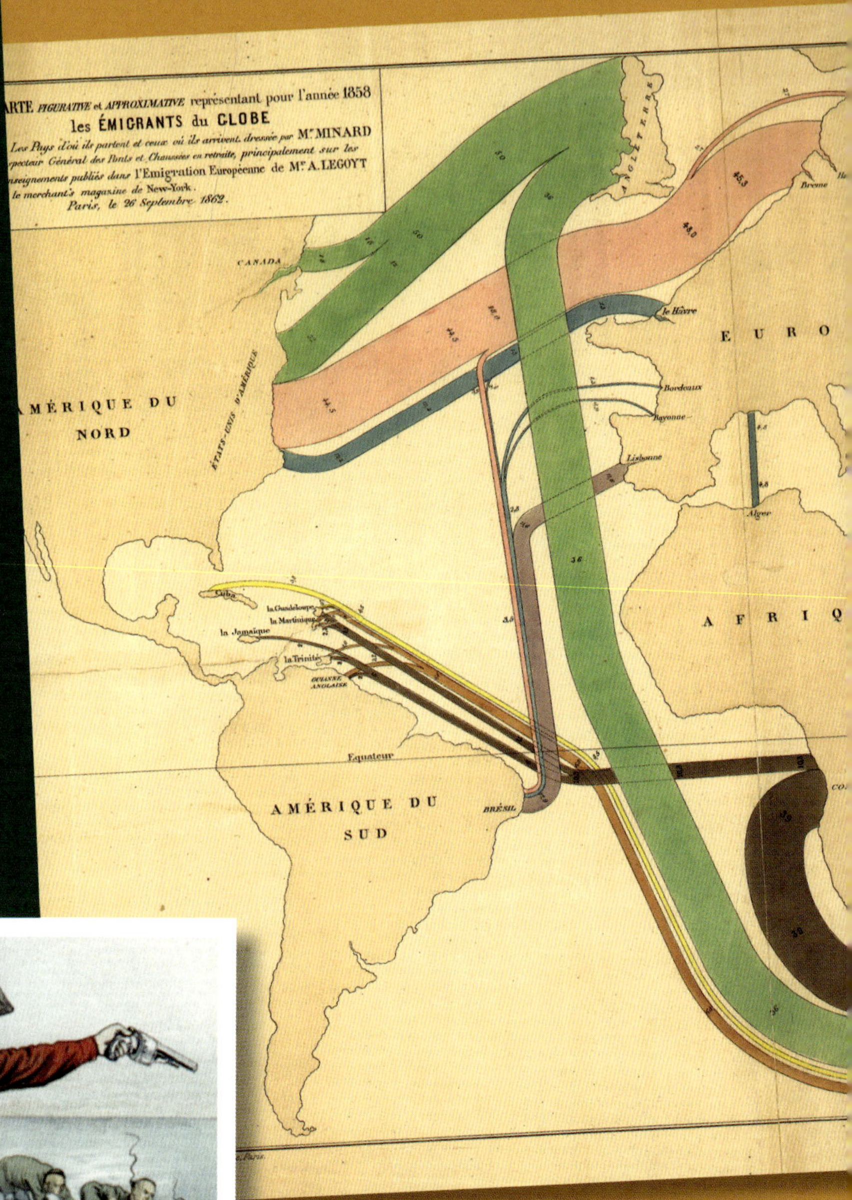

This political cartoon shows how some people felt about Chinese immigrants.

Mad About Immigration

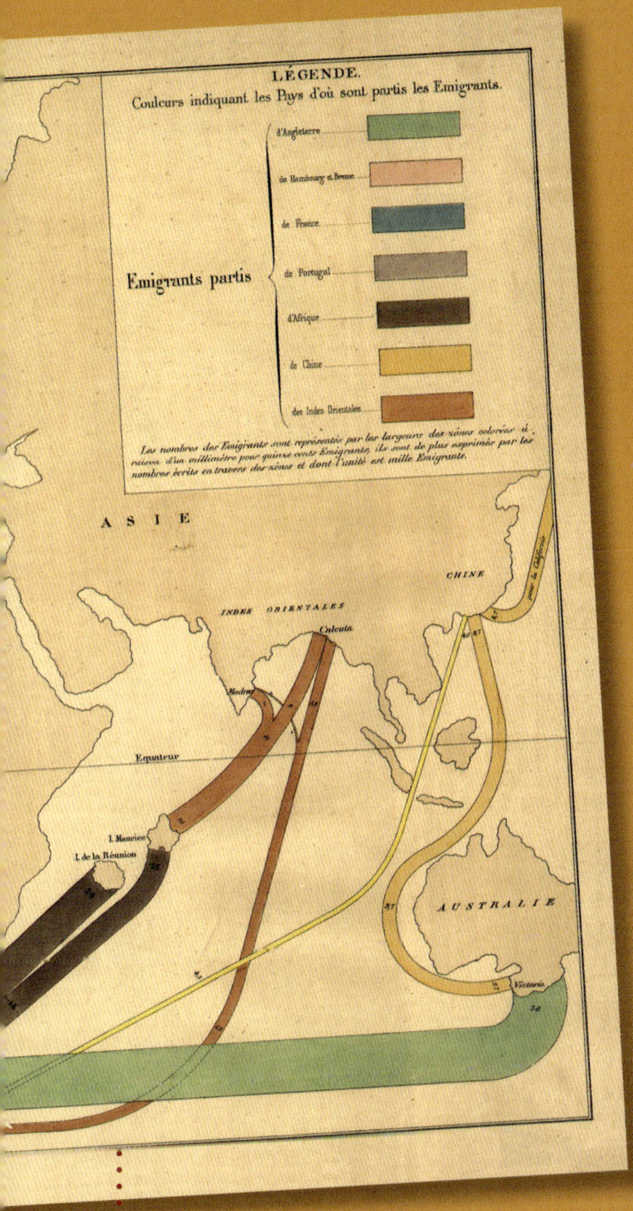

This French map shows immigration statistics in 1858.

During the late 1850s, United States citizens started to protest. They did not like so many people coming into their nation. They demanded action. The first immigration restrictions were in place by 1875. That's when Congress passed a law to keep out people with criminal records.

Seven years later, Congress passed a bill to halt Chinese immigration. At this time, Congress also put more limitations on all immigrants. People who were ill, insane, or who could not support themselves were not let in.

After 1917, each immigrant had to show the ability to read and write in his or her own language. That same year, Congress made a law barring all people from Asia and the Pacific islands. Filipinos from the Philippines were the only exception. The Philippines was a U.S. territory at that time. So they were not considered foreigners.

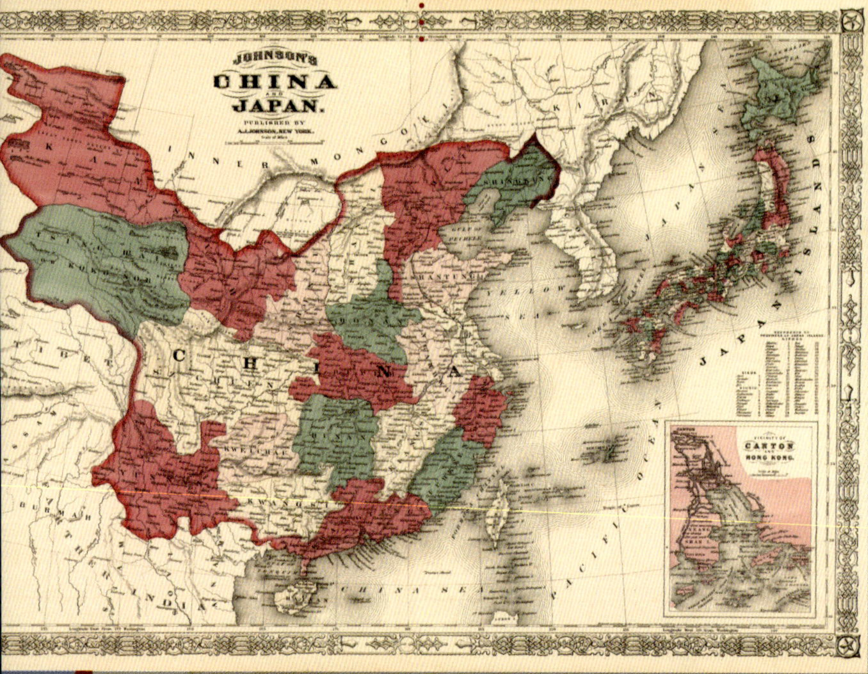

China in 1869

The Asian Experience

In 1882 Congress stopped Chinese immigration with the Chinese Exclusion Act. After that, fewer Asians tried to enter the nation. Then, in April 1906, an earthquake and fire tore through San Francisco. All legal records were lost. This left no way to prove who was a United States citizen.

Many Chinese men living there jumped at this chance. They claimed they were born in the United States. This made them and their children American citizens. It did not matter that the children had been born in China. Chinese men urged their families to rush to America.

These images show the destruction from the San Francisco earthquake of 1906.

To stop the Chinese **influx** (IN-fluhkz), the Angel Island Immigration Station opened in 1910. It is located in the San Francisco Bay.

Coming through this immigration station was difficult. When a ship sailed into port, people were grouped by nationality. Whites and those in first or second class got off in San Francisco. People with health problems and all Asians stayed aboard. They went to Angel Island.

Transcontinental Railroad

The Chinese did the most dangerous jobs for the railroads. They dug ditches, blasted tunnels through mountains, mined, and dammed rivers. In the 1870s, many employers decided not to hire Asians. So the resourceful Chinese opened restaurants and laundries.

Stuck on the Ship

The Bureau of Immigration processed passengers in this order: first class, second class, and **steerage**. Steerage was the lowest deck on the ship. After weeks at sea, the people in steerage were eager to get off the dirty, crowded ships.

Paper Sons

Some Chinese boys who wanted to come to the United States became "paper sons." Their parents bought papers which stated that they were children of American citizens. These boys had to memorize details about people they had never met to pass the questioning.

Exceptions to the Rules

Some Asians could enter America under the Chinese Exclusion Act of 1882. They were merchants, **clergy**, **diplomats**, teachers, and students.

Chinese boys wait for medical exams at Angel Island.

Angel Island Immigration Station is near San Francisco, California.

Angel Island Was Not Heaven

On Angel Island the officials detained all Chinese people. The buildings were hot and filthy. People stayed in small, smelly cells. The cells looked like zoo cages. The people were kept locked in and rarely went outdoors.

Guards threw small amounts of food on the floor for them to eat. Some lived in these horrid conditions for months before being questioned.

Each immigrant faced a Board of Special Inquiry. The majority of the board members had to vote yes for a person to be admitted to the United States. The board asked questions about the person's home life, family background, and village.

The immigrants had to prove that they belonged to American citizens. The U.S. citizens then had to answer the questions, too. If the answers from both people were not the same, the inspectors rejected the new immigrants. About 10 percent of all the immigrants were excluded.

Only a Few Allowed

In 1921, Congress limited the total number of people who could immigrate to the United States each year. These laws are known as **quotas** (KWOH-tuhz). Many members of Congress were from Germany, Great Britain, Scotland, and Ireland. So, they made laws that favored people from Europe. The quotas cut back on the number of people who could come from other places around the world.

The National Origins Act went into effect in 1924. This law set new quotas. Quotas for eastern Europe were much lower than before. But after this law, few Asians could immigrate to the United States.

Chinese workers canned salmon on the West Coast.

Dalip Singh Saund

World War II took many U.S. soldiers overseas to fight. While away at war, some of them got married. The War Brides Act of 1945 let them bring their spouses and children into the country. In 1952, the Immigration and Nationality Act set new quotas. These acts finally let people in from Asian nations and other places where immigrants had been blocked. Citizenship was finally offered to many Asian immigrants.

The Immigration Act of 1921 limited the number of people allowed in the United States.

A Success Story

Dalip Singh Saund (DAY-lip SING SAWND) came from India. He worked to get the government to end discrimination against Asians. He was the first Asian elected to the House of Representatives.

Unfair Laws

Despite the fact that the Chinese were hard working and did many of the jobs no one else wanted to do, people disliked them. By the 1920s, U.S. laws said that no Asian immigrants could own land, become U.S. citizens, or marry white people. It took a long time for these unfair laws to be changed.

Father Flanagan

Father Edward Flanagan arrived from Ireland in 1904. He created Boys' Town, a home for orphaned boys. His hard work and love helped thousands of children.

World Famous Architect

I.M. Pei (PAY) arrived as a Chinese student in 1935. This architect designed many famous buildings. He even created an addition for France's Louvre (LOO-vruh). This is the most famous art museum in the world.

Famous in America

Emigrants from other countries made important contributions to the nation. Most of their names have been forgotten. But a few gained fame. Elijah McCoy came to the United States from Canada in 1870. His parents lived there after escaping from slavery. He invented a lubricating cup. It improved steam engines and factory machinery.

Madeleine Albright came to the United States from Czechoslovakia (chek-uh-slow-VAW-kee-uh) in 1948. She was just eleven years old. As an adult, Albright became a United Nations ambassador. Then, in 1997, she became the first female secretary of state. She was very successful in this position for four years.

Chien-Shiung Wu (chee-en-SHE-uhng WOO) graduated from college in China. She immigrated to the United States in 1936. There, she earned two more college degrees. She then became a college professor. Wu was asked by the U.S. government to help build the atomic bomb. She is known as one of the most important women in science.

Madeleine Albright was the first female secretary of state.

Irving Berlin was a famous composer who immigrated to the United States. His family came from Russia. He composed "White Christmas" and "God Bless America."

Cultural Mosaic

America is a mix of many cultures. No place else on Earth has had so many immigrants. Each year about one million new people arrive. Many still settle in New York City.

In 1965, Congress lifted the limits it had put on immigration during the 1920s. As a result, in the past 40 years another 25 million people have come to the United States. Today, most immigrants come from Mexico, the Philippines, Russia, and China.

Immigration has not been easy, but it has brought new ideas to the places where the newcomers settled. Each group added to the whole country in its own way. These contributions include the food we eat, the way we speak, the music we love, and even the values we hold dear—like freedom of speech. All of these are based on the **assimilation** (uh-SIM-uh-lay-shuhn) of ideas from around the world. In so many ways, immigrants have made the United States what it is today.

Can You Believe It?

More than 100 different languages are spoken in New York City!

Questions for the Future

Many of the same questions that have been discussed for a century continue to be debated. Who should be allowed to come into America? Who should be excluded? And what should be done about the millions of immigrants who come into the country illegally each year?

Glossary

ancestor—someone who comes earlier in a family, such as a great-grandmother

assimilation—absorbed and incorporated (added to)

clergy—people trained to lead religious services, such as priests, rabbis, and ministers

crooked—criminal-like

detained—held for questioning

diplomats—people representing their nations' governments in foreign countries

emigrants—people who leave their nations to live somewhere new

emigrate—leave a place of residence to live somewhere new

ethnicities—belonging to particular nations or ethnic (cultural) groups

excluded—kept someone from being part of something

exploited—treated poorly

famine—extreme lack of food

harassed—created an unpleasant situation by repeated attacks

immigrants—people who come to new nations to live

immigrated—moved to a new place of residence

influx—the arrival of large numbers of people

insane asylums—special hospitals where those who are mentally ill go for treatment

interpreters—people trained to translate one language to another

irrevocable—unable to be changed or recovered

meager—barely enough

migrated—moved from one region or nation to another

piecework—work where wages are earned based on the number of pieces sewed

pogroms—organized killings of groups of people for political or religious reasons; usually planned by government leaders

quotas—fixed numbers or amounts

refuse—unwanted; trash

steerage—the lowest deck on a ship

swindlers—people who cheat others out of money or property

tempest-tost—tossed in a storm at sea

tenements—run-down apartment buildings in poor sections of cities

yearning—to feel an eager desire

Index

Image Credits

cover Bettmann/Corbis; p.1 Bettmann/Corbis; pp.4–5 Bettmann/Corbis; p.5 (left) Steamships.org; p.5 (right) Arvind Balaraman/Shutterstock, Inc.; p.6 (top) The Library of Congress; p.6 (bottom) Steamships.org; p.7 Steamships.org; pp. 8–9 Corbis; p.9 (top) The Library of Congress; p.9 (bottom) Bettmann/Corbis; p.10 The Library of Congress; p.10–11 The Granger Collection, New York; pp.12–13 The Granger Collection, New York; p.13 The Library of Congress; p.14 (top) The Library of Congress; p.14 (bottom) The Library of Congress; p.15 The Library of Congress; pp.16–17 The Library of Congress; p.17 Tony Spuria/ Shutterstock, Inc.; p.18 The Library of Congress; pp.18–19 The Library of Congress; p.20 The Library of Congress; pp.20–21 The Library of Congress; p.21 The Library of Congress; p.22 The Granger Collection, New York; pp.22–23 The Library of Congress; p.24 The Library of Congress; p.25 (left) The Granger Collection, New York; p.25 (right) Getty Images; p.26 Girls and Boys Town Hall of History Collection; p.27 (top) Reuters/ Corbis; p.27 (bottom) The Library of Congress; p.28 Keith Murphy/Shutterstock, Inc.; p.29 Steven Dern/Shutterstock, Inc.